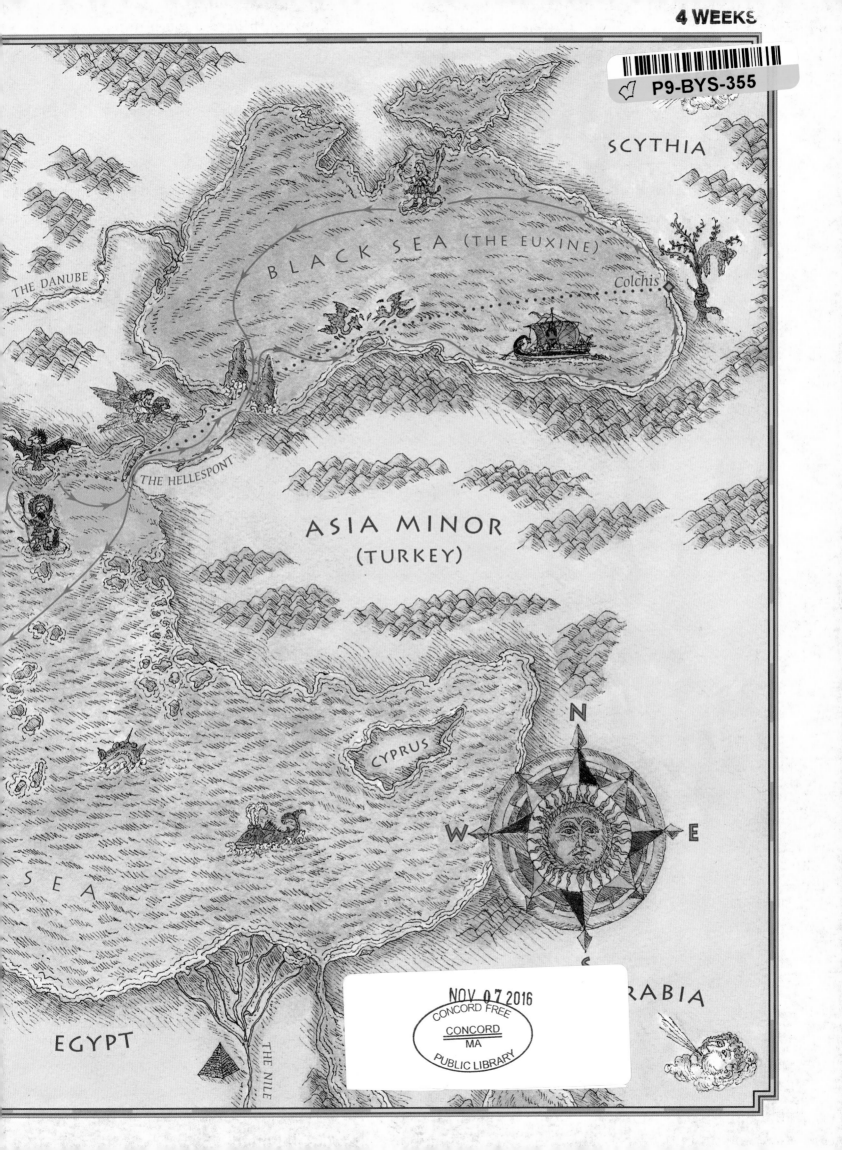

SCYTHIA

BLACK SEA (THE EUXINE)

THE DANUBE

Colchis

THE HELLESPONT

ASIA MINOR
(TURKEY)

CYPRUS

N

W E

S

SEA

EGYPT

THE NILE

RABIA

This one is for the boys, John and Ben.

DIAL BOOKS FOR YOUNG READERS
Penguin Young Readers Group • An imprint of Penguin Random House LLC
375 Hudson Street, New York, New York 10014, U.S.A.

Copyright © 2016 by Robert Byrd • Penguin supports copyright. Copyright fuels creativity, encourages diverse voices, promotes free speech, and creates a vibrant culture. Thank you for buying an authorized edition of this book and for complying with copyright laws by not reproducing, scanning, or distributing any part of it in any form without permission. You are supporting writers and allowing Penguin to continue to publish books for every reader.

Library of Congress Cataloging-in-Publication Data
Names: Byrd, Robert, author. • Title: Jason and the Argonauts / by Robert Byrd.
Description: New York : Dial Books for Young Readers, 2016. • Identifiers: LCCN 2015040910 | ISBN 9780803741188 (hardcover)
Subjects: LCSH: Jason (Greek mythology)—Juvenile literature. | Argonauts (Greek mythology)—Juvenile literature.
Classification: LCC BL820.A8 B97 2016 | DDC 398.20938/02—dc23 LC record available at http://lccn.loc.gov/2015040910

Manufactured in China on acid-free paper • 10 9 8 7 6 5 4 3 2 1
Text set in Sierra Com. and Lithos • The artwork was created using ink line, watercolor,
and colored inks on 140 lb. coldpress Arches watercolor paper.

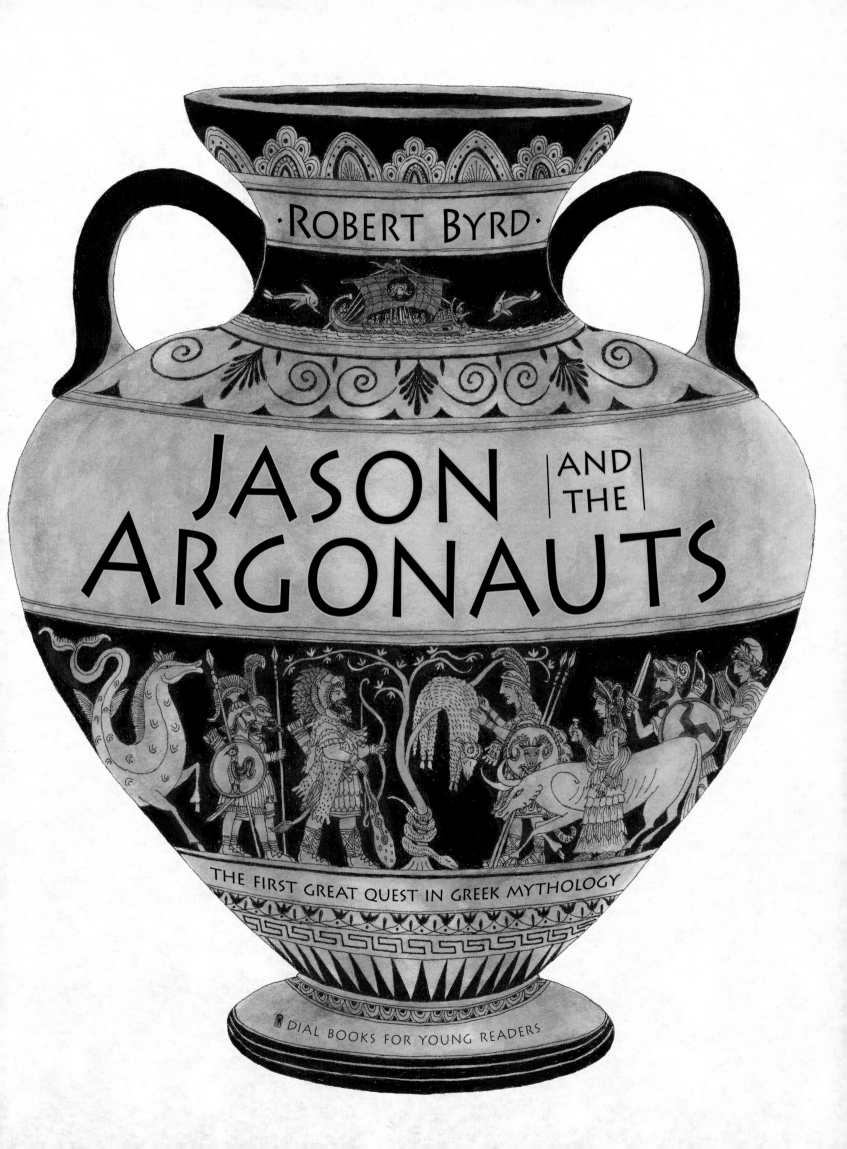

· ROBERT BYRD ·

JASON AND THE ARGONAUTS

THE FIRST GREAT QUEST IN GREEK MYTHOLOGY

DIAL BOOKS FOR YOUNG READERS

INTRODUCTION

THIS IS THE STORY OF A HERO, JASON, who lived many years ago in ancient Greece. He built a ship, filled it with other heroes willing to join him, and set out on an epic quest. His is a tale of gods and mortals, of adventure and danger, and, of course, glory.

The legend of Jason and the Argonauts is one of the oldest recorded tales in the Western world, and Jason himself was one of ancient Greece's first heroes. His quest was to retrieve the Golden Fleece. A fleece is the coat of a sheep, but this wasn't just any coat of wool—it was golden, and it came from a sheep that could fly, sent by the gods, and thought to have magical powers. This story is full of wonders: not only a flying sheep, but also fire-breathing bulls, a many-headed monster, a serpent who never sleeps, and men turned into beasts. Greedy kings hungry for power and riches, murderous queens, scheming magicians, and a wondrous ship to brave the dangers of the high seas—you will encounter all these in this book about Jason's quest.

You will meet gods, too, because Jason's story is not one of mortals alone. Though he was mortal, Jason was the descendant of immortal ancestors—the mighty gods of Olympus! The Greeks believed that the gods took great interest in the lives of mortals, especially heroes. They influenced and interfered—they had control over humanity's fate, and they had the forces necessary to alter events. They looked like people and appeared among humans and spoke to them. But they were not human—they acted and caused events to happen. Though they were thought to have great authority and wisdom, the gods also had very human characteristics. Prone to jealousy, selfishness, and vanity, they could be impulsive and vengeful. They would take sides; they would punish and reward. Woe to those who angered or competed with or disrespected the gods. Their wrath would come down quickly.

Every step of Jason's epic quest to retrieve the Golden Fleece was, in some way, shaped by the will of the gods. It was only with their help—and despite their hindrance—that Jason and his men were able to bring back the prize and claim legendary fame and fortune.

Jason's may have been the first recorded epic quest to come down to us among the myths of the ancient Greeks. But its age hasn't dimmed its power to draw us into the adventure. The story's characters stay clear, sharply etched, and real to us, whether they are gods or mortals. The myths of the Greeks are stories that enthrall us still and make the ancient past seem not so very far away.

THE GOLDEN FLEECE

ㄹㄹ

LONG BEFORE JASON WAS BORN, King Athamas ruled in central Greece. His wife, Nephele, a cloud nymph, bore him two children, a boy and a girl called Phrixus and Helle. But then she returned to the sky.

Athamas married an evil queen, who became insanely jealous of his children and plotted their end. She poisoned the crop seeds and caused a terrible famine. Then she lied, telling the king that a priestess from the Oracle of Delphi had proclaimed that he must sacrifice his children to end the famine and save his people. With great sorrow, Athamas agreed, but before this could happen Nephele came to her children's aid and begged Zeus to save them. He sent a winged golden ram—a prized gift from Hermes—to carry them to safety over land and sea. The children were told not to look down, but Helle did. While the wind whipped the waves around, she lost her grip and fell into the water and was lost. The straits she was flying over were forever after called the Hellespont, in her name.

The golden ram carried Phrixus on to a land called Colchis, on the very edge of the world. Aeetes,

the king of Colchis, welcomed them, but the ram asked to be sacrificed to the gods. Phrixus gave the golden fleece, the coat of the ram, to King Aeetes. In gratitude and to honor Zeus, the king placed the fleece in a sacred oak grove, guarded by a fearsome poisonous serpent that never slept. The Golden Fleece became the most prized treasure in the ancient world.

⚜ ZEUS ⚜

Zeus was the most important of the Greek gods. He reigned as the king of the gods on Mount Olympus. As the god of the sky and weather, he could control lightning and used it as a weapon. He was the god of escape and the patron of hospitality and the avenger of any guest treated poorly. Zeus had many children, both mortal and immortal.

THE ORACLE AT DELPHI was a priestess who was believed to speak for the god Apollo. She sat on a three-legged chair over a chasm and delivered prophesies while in a trancelike state. Ancient Greeks had complete faith in the oracle's words, even though their meaning was often unclear.

THE CAVE OF CHIRON

JASON WAS THE SON OF AESON, the rightful king of Iolcus. When Jason was a baby his wicked uncle, Pelias, the king's brother, took the throne unlawfully from Aeson. Jason's mother feared Pelias would harm the child so she sent him away, where he could be raised and taught in safety by the wise Chiron, king of the centaurs.

No child of Greece would ever have a teacher as learned as Chiron. He trained Jason well, in all the arts and in warfare. Chiron taught Jason the laws of nature and about the ways of the gods. When Jason was twenty, and could learn no more from Chiron, he left the cave to return to Iolcus and reclaim the throne in his father's name. After he said good-bye to the great centaur, he made his way down the forested slope until he came to a rapidly rushing stream. A very old woman stood there, afraid to cross.

Jason offered to carry her. He easily lifted her up and started across, but with every step she became heavier, and Jason stumbled through the water, losing a sandal on the way before barely reaching the other side. He was astonished then to see her disappear in a flash of light and to

hear a woman's voice. "Have no fear, Jason," she spoke. "I am Hera, wife of mighty Zeus, and you have undergone a trial. A true king must have compassion as well as wisdom and strength, and you have shown you possess all three. I will guide you through many difficult times to come."

She then bade him to present himself to his evil uncle Pelias just as he was. "You will understand when you look on the unworthy face of Pelias, who refuses to honor Zeus. A prophecy has told him he will lose his kingdom to one who will arrive wearing only one sandal. Go then," she continued. "Trust in me and let things happen as they will." And the voice was gone.

Stunned, Jason traveled on to Iolcus, clad in a leopard's skin, with two spears and his one sandal. At the king's palace the nobles stared at him with bold curiosity, but King Pelias trembled in fear when he saw him, remembering the words of the prophecy.

"Who are you?" demanded Pelias. "Why have you come?"

Jason stood tall and replied, "I am Jason, the son of Aeson, your brother, and I am here to claim the throne from you. For you have unjustly taken it."

Pelias had no intention of giving up his throne. Instead he was already thinking he would send this handsome youth on an impossible quest. "If you are truly the son of a king, you must demonstrate your worthiness. Bring me back the Golden Fleece, and you can have the throne." Pelias was sure no one could survive the long, dangerous journey to Colchis, much less the monstrous serpent guarding the Fleece. "Do this," Pelias went on, "and I will take it as a sign from the gods that you shall rule as king."

CENTAURS were half-man, half-horse creatures. They were believed to be wild and lawless beasts that fought with tree branches. Jason's civilized and educated teacher, Chiron, was the one exception.

HERA

Hera was the queen of the gods and the goddess of women and marriage. Because of her exceptional beauty, she was extremely vain and attacked anyone who slighted her appearance. Hera acted as Jason's special protector during his quest. Her symbol was the peacock.

THE SPEAKING TREE

THE GOLDEN FLEECE! The very words thrilled Jason. To bring back the Golden Fleece would give him fame and glory and stand him high in the eyes of the gods. But he also knew such an epic adventure would hold tremendous danger for anyone who would dare undertake it, and that he surely would need help.

He went to seek advice from the oracle at Dodona, a towering oak tree, sacred to Zeus. Jason stood nervously before the old tree, and asked, "What must I do to gain the Golden Fleece?" The tree stood silent, and then its branches and leaves gradually began to move, and it spoke in a deep and raspy voice.

"First, find Argus, the builder of ships, and have him build a boat with oars for fifty men."

Jason sought out Argus, who agreed to build the best ship that had ever set sail from Iolcus. No ship this large had ever been built before, and crowds gathered to watch, amazed by the size and beauty of the vessel, which was named *Argo*.

Jason then made one more trip to the great oak, and once more the tree spoke. "Take this branch," it commanded, stretching out a powerful limb, "and cut from it the figurehead for the *Argo*." Jason found the finest woodworker in Iolcus, and when he began to carve the branch his hands moved swiftly over the wood. Then magically from the branch there appeared the form of a woman wearing a golden helmet, with her arm extended, pointing ahead. As the builder fit her into the ship's prow, Jason was startled to see her eyes and lips move, and she spoke:

"Now gather your crew, Jason. Find the best, the bravest, the strongest, and the most cunning—the greatest heroes in all Greece." The voice was Hera's. But only Jason could hear her—he alone would have the privilege of conversing with so powerful a goddess as Hera, who would guide him on his quest.

ZEUS AND HERA

Although they were husband and wife, Zeus and Hera fought often. Hera was always jealous of Zeus's many mistresses and took her revenge by tormenting them, goddesses and mortals alike. Hera also sought vengeance against their children, including the famous hero Hercules. During Jason's journey, Hera sought help for him from time to time from her powerful husband.

THE HEROES GATHER

THE HEROES WHO ANSWERED THE CALL were the finest Greece had to offer. Many were endowed with phenomenal superhuman powers. They descended on Iolcus in high spirits, all eager to claim their part and to proclaim their loyalty to Jason and the quest. There were kings, princes and noblemen, warriors, sages, and the sons of gods and goddesses.

Hercules was the most powerful and fearsome of all the Greek heroes, and the strongest man who had ever lived. When Jason heard that he was on his way to join the expedition, he was apprehensive. He knew that Hercules would be of great value, but he did not want Hercules's glory to overshadow his. He also knew that Hercules's violent temper was unpredictable.

When Jason first encountered Hercules, he was astonished by his enormous size and frightening appearance. He thought it best to flatter Hercules, and asked him if he would like to lead the crew. Hercules then told Jason that he, too, had once been a pupil of the centaur Chiron, and that Chiron had recently come to him in a dream and said that Jason was better suited to lead the Argonauts. Hercules would accompany Jason as a member of the crew. Jason accepted this arrangement, but several of the Argonauts opposed it. They complained that Hercules's great bulk would cause the *Argo* to ride unevenly. This talk ended quickly, however, when Hercules waved his massive club and threatened to crack a few skulls

NOTABLE ARGONAUTS

Many of the Argonauts were gifted with exceptional physical and mental powers.

CALAIS AND ZETES | The winged sons of the North Wind. They could fly as high and fast and far as the four winds.

ORPHEUS | He could charm humans and beasts with his lyre, and cause trees, plants, and rocks to dance.

ATALANTA | The only female Argonaut. Raised by a bear, she grew up to be a famed hunter and the fastest runner in Greece.

ANCAEUS | The strongest Argonaut, after Hercules. He wore a bearskin and carried a double-sided axe called a labrys.

MELEAGER | The warrior and hunter who fought and killed the ravaging Calydonian boar. He was in love with Atalanta.

PERICLYMENUS | The shape-shifter. In battle he could turn himself into a lion, a snake, a swan, ants, or a swarm of bees.

EUPHEMUS | A great swimmer who could walk and run on water without getting wet.

NESTOR | The oldest and wisest Argonaut, he fought in the Trojan War at the age of 110. Jason sought his counsel.

MOPSUS | He could predict the future, had unerring wisdom, and could understand the language of birds.

LYNCEUS | The *Argo*'s lookout. He was so sharp-sighted he could see nine miles away, and through trees, rocks, and the earth.

TIPHYS | The *Argo*'s helmsman. He could predict rising waves and storm winds by reading the sun, moon, and stars.

THESEUS | A king who, as a boy, fought and killed the murderous half-man, half-bull Minotaur.

THE ARGO SETS SAIL

JASON WAS PLEASED WITH THE BEAUTIFUL SHIP and his renowned crew, and he strode through Iolcus to rousing cheers. But some in the crowds greeted him with cries of lament, and threw scarlet windflowers in his path, a symbol of those who die young. Iphias, the chief priestess, stopped him to offer prayers of safety, but Jason could only think of the glorious voyage that lay ahead, and he rudely brushed her aside. "That insolent young man," she muttered bitterly. "May he remember me when that proud ship of his lies a rotting skeleton on the beach."

Jason was responsible for the provisions on the *Argo*, but many of the Argonauts were wealthy and paid their own way, bringing sacks of grain, sides of cured beef, fig bread, sundried grapes, roasted salted filberts, jars of honey, and honey cakes flavored with thyme and pine kernels. The ship also carried water, wine, olive oil, dolphin oil, barley bread, and pickled foods. The Argonauts had their own arms, armor, and bedding, and each had his own storage locker under his seat. The *Argo* carried spare rope, sails, and tools.

When the ship was ready, a great wailing arose from the people. Some were real cries of grief at the

dangers these men might face on such a perilous voyage, but much of the carrying on came from mourners who were hired by the Argonauts to avoid jealousy by any god who might feel antagonistic toward the ship or crew.

When the *Argo* was finally ready to sail, the Argonauts found the ship too heavy to move off the beach. Jason turned to the figurehead, and Hera spoke again. "Jason, have the men board the ship with oars held up high. Then have Orpheus play his lyre." Orpheus played, and the ship began to slide forward. The melody quickened, and the galley swiftly slipped into the sea. A loud cheer erupted from the crew as the *Argo* was launched on the most momentous sea journey ever ventured.

Poseidon smiled and called on Zephyrus, the god of the West Wind, to give the Argonauts a strong breeze. The *Argo* sailed smoothly into the Aegean Sea, heading east.

POSEIDON

Poseidon was the god of the sea, the creator of horses, and the protector of all waters. He was considered the most powerful god after his brother, Zeus. Sometimes called the Earth Shaker, Poseidon's violent temper caused earthquakes, storms at sea, and volcanic eruptions. His unpredictable personality could determine the fate of ships and sailors. He was married to Amphitrite, a sea goddess.

GREEK SHIPS preferred to sail close to land, in order to restock at ports along the way. Unsure what goods would be available in strange ports, they carried their own provisions as well: wine, oil, honey, olives, sacks of grains, hard cheeses, and fresh water. Liquids were stored in amphorae, or large earthenware vessels, which were lined up on either side of the keel as ballast, to keep the ship balanced.

HERCULES, OUR SHIPMATE

SO BEGAN THEIR ADVENTURES with the gods challenging the Argonauts with many trials. They sailed over the Aegean Sea to Bear Island, where King Cyzicus welcomed them with a feast. Jason could see that the king did not seem to be enjoying the festivities and asked him what was wrong. "We are constantly besieged by savages from the next mountain who harass my people and destroy everything," Cyzicus said. "They are giants, each with six arms, and carry a different weapon in each hand, which are like the paws on bears." Lynceus, the Argonaut with the keenest eyes, looked toward the mountain and could see these giants sneaking down the mountainside toward the harbor where Hercules and a few of the Argonauts had volunteered to guard the *Argo*.

Jason and the rest of his band hurried to get their arms and return to the ship, but before they could reach it the giants were rushing the *Argo* and throwing large boulders at it. Hercules possessed such phenomenal strength that he was able to block the stones, and he and his men held on until Jason and the rest arrived and destroyed most of the giants with bows and arrows. The other ogres ran away, and never returned. King Cyzicus was very grateful, and he sent the *Argo* off with a full store of supplies.

They sailed to Chios next, but on the way Jason and Hercules engaged in a rowing duel. Jason passed out and Hercules broke his oar, so no winner was declared. When they landed, Hercules went to find wood for a new oar. His young attendant, Hylas, accompanied him. But Hylas was kidnapped by nymphs and pulled down into a pool of water. Hercules searched for Hylas all night, stomping and crashing through the woods, but he never found him, and drove himself mad at the loss of his friend.

When Hercules lost his senses he was a terrifying figure to confront, and the Argonauts feared his great destructive power. Urged on by Calais and Zetes, the men voted to sail without him, and Hercules, distraught, returned to his Labors.

LABORS OF HERCULES

Hercules, the strongest man who ever lived, was the son of Zeus and a mortal, and he was hated by Hera. His passionate emotions frequently got him in trouble. Once when it was extremely hot, he threatened to shoot the sun with a bow and arrow. Many of his famous exploits were the result of punishment for acts due to his anger. The most well known are his Twelve Labors. Hera made him lose his mind for a time, and he murdered his wife and children. To atone for this, he had to perform twelve nearly impossible tasks. He was made to kill beasts and monsters, including a ferocious boar and a nine-headed hydra. It took him a year to catch a fleet-footed deer and bring it back alive. He cleaned a huge stable full of bulls by diverting two rivers so the waters would wash through the building. The last and most difficult of his tasks was to go to the underworld and capture with his bare hands Cerberus, a monster with three heads and a body covered with poisonous snakes. These Labors took Hercules twelve years to complete. He was the only mortal to become a god at his death.

PHINEAS AND THE HARPIES

THE ARGONAUTS SAILED NEXT to a small island near Thrace where they came upon poor King Phineas, a soothsayer. Zeus had been angered by Phineas's amazing ability to tell the future too clearly, a gift he had received from Apollo, who was feuding with Zeus. To punish him, Zeus caused Phineas to go blind and drove him into exile. He was so thin and weak he could hardly stand, and he begged Jason for help. Whenever food was put before Phineas, he was set upon by harpies, who would sweep down and steal it. The harpies were vile creatures with the heads of witches, bodies of vultures, and the wings of bats. Poor Phineas was helpless to resist them.

Jason set some fruit and nuts before Phineas and sure enough, the harpies attacked and stole the food. So Jason sent Calais and Zetes, the winged sons of Boreas, after the harpies, and with drawn swords they drove them for a hundred miles across the sky. Iris, the goddess of the rainbow, came between them and asked the two brothers to spare the harpies, promising they would never bother Phineas again.

Jason was able to heal Phineas's blindness, remembering a medicinal cure he learned from Chiron. Then he asked Phineas if he knew the best way to reach Colchis. The grateful Phineas told him there was really only one way, and it was most dangerous.

IRIS

Iris was the goddess of the rainbow, and a messenger to the Olympian gods. She held a herald's staff and a vase filled with water from the River Styx, which she could use to put liars into a deep sleep for a full year.

HARPIES were the demonic spirits of strong wind gusts. They were called the hounds of Zeus, and were known to harass mortals if bidden by the gods.

THE CLASHING ROCKS

"**Y**OU MUST PASS through the Symplegades, or Clashing Rocks, two huge boulders that continually smash into each other," Phineas emphasized. "When the *Argo* gets close enough, send a dove to fly between them, and as it passes through, the rocks will pull back as they always do, ready to smash together again. At that one instant, you must row for your lives." Then he said to Jason, "And when you do reach Colchis, trust in Aphrodite."

The Argonauts left Phineas in peace and sailed until Lynceus spied land ahead, with the two huge boulders guarding the passageway, and the waves crashing and foaming around them.

Suddenly, the anxious rowers let out a cheer as a heron, a bird sacred to the goddess Athena, and an omen of good fortune, flew overhead. But the cheers quickly turned to cries of anguish as a hawk swooped down to attack the heron, just missing. As the hawk turned to strike again, Phalerus, an Argonaut skilled with bow and arrow, took aim and brought it down with a single shot. The omen was preserved.

The water turned rough and waves rocked the ship, and Tiphys, the helmsman, could barely hold his course. But the *Argo* moved toward the great shifting stones.

Jason then released the dove, and just as it flew through the narrow passage the rocks closed. The dove got by, losing only two tail feathers. Then the Argonauts rowed as never before, and when the stones pulled back, the *Argo* raced through the gap before it closed, the first ship ever to do so. They suffered only scratches on the stern, and the rocks were locked in place, never again to move, for it was the will of the gods that the rocks should be frozen once a mortal had passed through.

ATHENA

Athena was the goddess of wisdom, war, justice, and the arts. A daughter of Zeus, she burst from his head fully formed and clad in armor. She aided armies whose causes were true and lent aid to artists and craftspeople. Her symbols were the owl and the olive branch.

THE STYMPHALIAN BIRDS

AFTER NAVIGATING SAFELY THROUGH the straits of the Hellespont and the Clashing Rocks, the Argonauts sailed into the open waters of the Euxine, known as the Black Sea. Following several days of smooth sailing, they stopped on a small island for fresh food and water. The men set up camp on the shore and were resting on the beach when a hail of metal arrows rained down on them. They could not tell where these strange, small arrows came from, as they had scouted the island and thought it uninhabited. Unbeknownst to the Argonauts, they had landed on the Isle of Ares, named for the god of war, and home to his pets, the man-eating Stymphalian birds. The birds had bronze beaks and claws, and metal dart-like arrows for feathers, which they were now shooting at the Argonauts. The men covered themselves with their shields and helmets, and Jason ran to the *Argo* to ask the figurehead for help.

Hera's voice told Jason to have the men bang their shields with their swords as loud and long as they could. When they did, such a great clamor rose up that the frightened birds panicked and flew off.

Greatly relieved, the Argonauts were returning to the *Argo*, when they found four exhausted men on the beach. They were princes, the four sons of Phrixus, who long ago had been saved by the flying golden ram.

These brothers had been shipwrecked in a storm and told Jason they could help him reach Colchis. There, King Aeetes, who kept the Golden Fleece, had turned into a cruel tyrant. The terrible serpent guarding it would kill anyone who came near the Golden Fleece.

Jason agreed to take the four princes with him, and the Argonauts now began the last stretch of this most extraordinary journey.

⇌ ARES ⇌

A res was the god of war and the son of Zeus and Hera. Whereas Athena represented the art of strategic warfare, he embodied the brutality of battle. Blood-thirsty and cruel, Ares was feared by mortals and disliked by the gods. He rode his war chariot with his two sons, Fear (Phobos) and Terror (Deimos).

THE ARGONAUTS ARRIVE IN COLCHIS

THE ARGONAUTS SAILED ALONG the coast of the Black Sea until they reached Colchis. King Aeetes was furious that strangers would dare land in his kingdom without permission, and when Jason was brought before him, he demanded to know why he was there. Jason announced that he had come to take back the Golden Fleece. King Aeetes had not the slightest intention to agree to this, as the Golden Fleece was his greatest prize. Carefully controlling his anger, the king said, "Well, young Jason, here you boldly trespass in my country, and then make such an absurd request. I find myself amused. But I admire your forthrightness, and I will grant you the Golden Fleece, if you can pass a test of your bravery. If not, you will die." Hera heard this and knew Jason would need some help.

During this discussion, King Aeetes's beautiful daughter Medea was standing by his side. Medea was a sorceress of great power. Hera asked Aphrodite to have Eros, her son, shoot an arrow of love into Medea's heart. When the arrow struck, Medea fell in love with Jason, and then and there she vowed to use her power to save Jason from her cold-blooded father.

Aeetes then told Jason the impossible test: "First you must tame and harness my fire-breathing bulls; then plough the field of Ares, and after that, plant a crop of dragon's teeth." Aeetes was sure that Jason could not survive these tasks. The two bulls were wild and gigantic, and their lungs

were iron furnaces forged by Hephaestus that shot out deadly flames. The dragon's teeth would immediately grow into an army that Jason would have to defeat.

Medea went to the Temple of Hecate for help. Hecate was a witch goddess, and she prepared a secret salve that would protect anyone who wore it from fire and iron, for one day only. Medea took the salve to Jason and told him to fear nothing, and in return Jason promised to take her away with him and be faithful to her always. Hera overheard his promise and approved.

In the morning Jason went to the bulls in the field of Ares. The salve also gave him new powers of strength. Despite their immense size and the blasts of their fiery breaths, Jason subdued them, seizing them by the horns and fixing them to the yoke and plough.

APHRODITE

Aphrodite was the goddess of love and beauty. The only Greek deity without parents, Aphrodite appeared in the sea atop a large scallop shell. Zeus worried that her beauty would cause the gods to fight over her, so he arranged for Aphrodite to marry his son, Hephaestus.

EROS was Aphrodite's impish son and the god of love and desire. He had wings and a quiver of golden arrows. When shot into the heart, his arrows caused mortals and gods alike to fall in love.

JASON AND THE EARTHBORN WARRIORS

THE BULLS RAGED AND ROARED AND SNORTED FIRE. But Jason prodded them on with his spear of iron, which was also covered with the miraculous strengthening salve. Then he ploughed the field for a full day. By night he sowed the furrows with the dragon's teeth he carried in his golden helmet. As soon as he planted a tooth, a gigantic armed warrior would sprout from the ground. When the field was filled with belligerent soldiers, Jason threw a boulder in their midst. Not knowing where it came from, the entire earthborn army turned on one another, slashing and hacking with their swords until none were left alive.

Jason was taken aback by the number of dead, but Medea told him, "Do not feel sorry, Jason. Men will always fight and die for empty causes, like glory, fame, and laurel wreaths. The Golden Fleece is now yours to take."

HEPHAESTUS

Hephaestus was the god of metalwork and fire. His parents were Zeus and Hera, and he worked as the blacksmith to the gods. He forged their thrones, armor, and weapons. Hephaestus was once cast out of Olympus and fell all the way to earth, injuring his legs. So, although Hephaestus was extremely strong, his legs remained weak.

THE DRAGON'S TEETH that Jason had to sow were from the sacred dragon of Ares, which was killed by a prince, Cadmus. Athena was angered by this and made him sow the teeth, which grew into vicious warriors, just as Jason's did. Athena gave the remaining dragon's teeth to Aeetes.

Jason Takes the Fleece

MEDEA THEN STEALTHILY led Jason into the sacred oak grove where the Golden Fleece hung from the branch of a large oak tree. How it gleamed in the moonlight! But it was guarded by the never-sleeping serpent, whose thick scaly coils were wrapped around the trunk of the tree. "Wait," whispered Medea, and she moved closer to the creature and began a slow mysterious chant. The great beast raised his head toward her, and she sprinkled its snout with a sleeping potion of Hecate's concoction she had hidden in her sleeve. The serpent fell asleep on the ground.

"Now!" she called out, and Jason quickly took the magnificent Fleece from the tree. The two ran to the beach where the *Argo* was moored. They boarded the ship and the Argonauts hastily rowed for the open waters of the sea.

When King Aeetes found out what happened he was filled with rage and sent his fleet of warships after Jason and Medea. The next day, Aeetes's fleet, led by his son Apsyrtus, caught up to the *Argo*. But Medea devised a plan to help them escape. She sent a message to her brother pretending she was sorry for her actions, and saying she wanted to return home. She asked Apsyrtus to secretly meet her on a nearby island. But she told Jason to lie in wait, and when her brother appeared, Jason jumped out from behind some bushes and brutally killed Apsyrtus. In confusion, the Colchian fleet dispersed, and the *Argo* sailed away safely with the Golden Fleece.

Hermes

Hermes was the messenger of the gods and the herald of Zeus, usually shown wearing winged sandals and carrying his herald's staff. He was the patron of athletic games. The ram was sacred to him, and he was the protector of shepherds. He gave Zeus the golden sheep who carried Phrixus to Colchis.

HECATE was a powerful goddess of witchcraft and magic, who was known to weave potent spells. She is associated with the dark side of the moon, and with mists. She is often shown at a crossroads.

CIRCE AND THE ISLAND OF THE SIRENS

THE MURDER OF APSYRTUS enraged the gods. Zeus, watching from Mount Oympus, proclaimed his fury and disgust at Jason and Medea's betrayal of her own flesh and blood. Hera, speaking through the figurehead, rebuked them. "You will not escape the wrath of Zeus," she cried out. "And you will endlessly roam the seas unless you seek out Circe, ask her forgiveness, and be purified of your crime."

The trip ahead was terrible. The Argonauts sailed through rough seas and howling storms to the island of Aeaea, the home of Circe, a frightful sorceress, who liked to turn men into animals. Medea instructed the crew to remain on board the *Argo*, and taking Jason's hand they walked ashore. They passed many odd-looking creatures with something strangely human about their appearance, and then entered Circe's chambers.

Circe listened to their pleas. She sacrificed unleavened cakes to Zeus, whom she called the Great Cleanser. Then she bid Jason and Medea each drink purified water from a golden goblet. Acting with Zeus's approval, she pardoned them for their crime, if Medea agreed to relinquish her powers of evil magic. Then Jason and Medea returned to the *Argo*.

Now the *Argo* passed by the island of the Sirens, beautiful creatures who lured sailors with their enchanting songs onto shore where their ships would be crushed on the rocks. The Sirens began to sing their bewitching songs and the Argonauts drifted helplessly toward the shore. But Medea urged Orpheus to play his harp and sing so beautifully and loud that he drowned out the song of the Sirens, and the *Argo* passed by unharmed.

CIRCE

Circe was an immortal sorceress and Medea's aunt, famed—and feared—for using her magic potions to turn men into beasts. She was exiled to Aeaea, the Island of the Dawn, for killing her husband. Circe was also responsible for turning a beautiful maiden named Scylla into a grotesque monster during a fit of jealousy.

SIRENS were half-bird, half-human women who lured sailors to their deaths with their beautiful singing. They were doomed to die if anyone ever heard their song and survived. When Orpheus's music overpowered their voices, they jumped into the sea and drowned; all except two, who had not sung with them.

SCYLLA AND CHARYBDIS

THE *ARGO* NOW HAD NO CHOICE but to pass through another narrow, rocky space, which was guarded by two grotesque and deadly creatures. On one side was Scylla, a ghoulish hag from the waist up, with a lower body formed like an immense fish, with six vicious, fanged dog heads, who ripped apart anyone who came near. On the other side, Charybdis waited, a monster with a gigantic, repulsive mouth, who was always hungry. She sucked into her stomach anything within her reach and created a violent and unceasing whirlpool the Argonauts would have to steer through.

The *Argo* floated like a cork in the crashing waves between these two, seemingly lost. Poseidon, who had been impressed by the courage and endurance of the crew, called on Thetis, the queen of the Nereids, to gather her sea nymphs. They rose up from the depths of the ocean, riding dolphins, and carried the *Argo* past the two hideous demons, over the churning water to the safety of the open sea.

⟫⟫⟫ THETIS ⟪

Thetis was a goddess of water, and queen of the fifty Nereids, or sea nymphs. The nymphs were the daughters of an ancient sea god and were considered minor deities. They protected sailors and were Poseidon's attendants.

LOST IN THE DESERT

THE SHIP HAD SMOOTH SAILING for two days until a terrifying storm struck. The wind and waves drove the *Argo* off course for nine days and nights, but then a massive wave threw the ship onto the desert sands of Libya. The land was hostile and inhabited only by venomous snakes. The Argonauts feared they would perish from heat and lack of water, but three goat-headed nymphs appeared to Jason in a dream and told him not to despair, that Poseidon would send him a sign. The next morning a large Hippocamp, half-horse and half-fish, appeared from nowhere in a mist. Nestor, the oldest of the Argonauts, spoke up, and said, "Jason, this is the sign from Poseidon. These fabulous beasts pull Poseidon's chariot, and this one will return to the sea, where it lives. We must follow it to water."

Hera then spoke from the prow of the *Argo*. "Nestor is right," she said. "You must follow the horse-fish to safety."

The Argonauts hoisted the *Argo* onto their shoulders and trailed after the Hippocamp, but the ship was heavy, and the going was slow, and the animal was soon out of sight.

The Argonauts followed the great beast's tracks in the sand for twelve days and nights, until a gusty sandstorm covered them over, and they thought they were doomed. But Calais and Zetes flew high enough to see the ocean in the distance, and in two more days, the weary crew reached the sea.

The Argonauts were now on their way home, with only the big island of Crete between them and Iolcus. Notus, the South Wind, gave them strong breezes, and they headed for the island, their last stop for food and water.

THE ANEMOI

The Anemoi were the gods of the four winds. Boreas was the North Wind, the god of cold and winter. (His twin sons were the winged Argonauts, Calais and Zetes.) Notus, the South Wind, brought heat and ruined crops. Eurus was the unlucky East Wind who brought warmth and rain. Zephryus was the gentle West Wind who caused plants to grow and thrive.

THE GOAT-HEADED NYMPHS symbolized the Triple Goddess—maiden, mother, and old woman— a common divinity in ancient cultures.

THE BRONZE GIANT

SEVERAL DAYS LATER they sighted land, but as the ship drew closer, huge boulders suddenly began bombarding them. Up ahead, a colossal figure stood onshore, hurling these stones at the ship. It was the bronze giant Talos who guarded the island.

Three times each day Talos walked completely around Crete, looking for anyone who would dare try to land. When he finally turned and began to stroll away Jason quickly brought the *Argo* to a beach in a hidden cove. The Argonauts hid behind rocks until Talos appeared again. But he spotted them and strode angrily forward. Medea began to chant powerful, unworldly incantations, and the menacing Talos gradually slowed down, and then stopped, as though in a deep trance. Medea snuck up behind him and very slowly pulled a plug from his ankle. At once the molten blood that kept Talos alive poured out on the beach, and the bronze giant collapsed in a huge heap, cold and still.

The Argonauts gathered food and water and hurriedly set sail from Crete. But, as darkness fell, the sky turned a solid black, so dark that the moon and every star disappeared. Not even Lynceus with his fantastic eyesight could catch a glimpse of Canopus, the *Argo*'s guiding star. The Argonauts drifted without direction, groping in the vast blackness. But ever watchful, Hera saved them again. She urged Apollo to send a beam of light so they could right their course and find their way home.

APOLLO

After his father Zeus, Apollo was the most revered god. He was the god of light, prophecy, truth, medicine, and music. Like his twin sister, Artemis, Apollo carried a bow. He also carried a lyre, which represented joy, through music, poetry, and dance.

THE ANCIENTS, like sailors through the ages, navigated by the stars. Canopus, the Argo's guiding star, was the brightest star in the skies above the Mediterranean.

THE ARGONAUTS COME HOME

JASON WAS GREETED with tragic news upon his arrival at Iolcus. A fisherman revealed to Jason that King Pelias had murdered his parents, and had sworn to kill him when he returned. This was not the welcome he had expected, so Jason had Medea fashion one of her devious schemes. Disguised as an ancient sorceress, she went to the palace and begged the guards to let her see the king. Medea told Pelias she had magic potions that could turn any living thing from old age to youth again. Pelias had aged, and he commanded the old woman to prove she could do it.

"Bring me a cauldron of boiling water and the oldest ram you have," she responded. Guards brought in the cauldron and the ram. She put the ram in the water and poured in some of the potion, and out jumped a playful young lamb. Pelias told her to make him young again, too, but Medea said that his daughters must put him in the cauldron and add the magic potion. When the daughters put Pelias in the cauldron nothing happened, for the potion that Medea gave them held no magic. The evil King Pelias died in the boiling water at the hands of his own children.

Jason was now revenged, and he placed the Golden Fleece in the Temple of Zeus and took back the throne. But the gods turned against Medea for having tricked Pelias's blameless daughters into murdering their own father. The people of Iolcus refused to accept Medea as their queen, and she and Jason were forced to leave.

They fled to Corinth and were welcomed by King Creon, but Jason's feelings toward Medea began to change. He now feared her magic and the awesome power she possessed. Forgetting everything she had done for him, he told Medea that he no longer loved her, and that he was going to marry Glauce, the daughter of King Creon, and inherit the throne. Medea, in rage and vengeance, then murdered the children she had with Jason, and escaped in a chariot pulled by two dragons sent by her grandfather, Helios, the sun god.

HELIOS

Helios was the god of the sun and one of the ancient Titans who ruled before the Olympians. Ancient Greeks believed that Helios drove the sun across the sky in a golden chariot pulled by golden winged stallions. He was the father of King Aeetes and Circe.

THE HERO'S END

JASON WAS DEVASTATED by the loss of his children, and he left Corinth. He had fallen out of favor with the gods, especially Hera, for breaking his promise to Medea. He wandered through Greece, homeless, forgotten by his friends, reliving his past glory and grieving for the tragedies that ruined him.

Many years later he returned to Iolcus, and walking on the shore he came upon the beached hull of the *Argo*, now rotten with age. He sat down under the prow of the old ship, resting in its shade, when the figurehead broke off and fell, killing him instantly.

Jason's story is a classic tale of bravery and valor, but also deceit, trickery, and vengeance. It shows how the whims of the gods played with the lives of mere mortals for their own pleasure and gain.

⊃ ARGO NAVIS ⊂

In Jason's time, the constellation Argo Navis could be seen in southern Mediterranean skies. The ancient Greeks believed it depicted the Argo, and the constellation's brightest star, Canopus, was thought to help navigate the ship on its quest for the Golden Fleece. Today, it can only be seen in the Southern Hemisphere.

T·H·E OLYMPIANS

ZEUS
The god of sky, thunder and lightning, weather and hospitality. He was the king of the gods and the father of several gods, goddesses, and mortal heroes.

ARTEMIS
The goddess of hunting, nature, wild beasts, and newborns. She was the protector of young women.

APOLLO
The god of music, truth, poetry, sun, and light. He was the prophetic god of the Oracle of Delphi.

HERA
The goddess of women and marriage. She was the queen of the gods, and was known for her jealous rage against her enemies and Zeus's many lovers.

POSEIDON
The god of the sea and horses. He was known as the bringer of earth-quakes and had a violent temper. Poseidon is often depicted holding a trident.

ATHENA
The goddess of wisdom, courage, law, justice, war, the arts, civilization, and religion. Athena burst into the world, fully grown, from Zeus's head.

DEMETER
The goddess of corn, grain, fruit, the harvest, and fertility of the earth. She presided over the cycle of life and death.

ARES
The god of war and the violence of combat. He was destructive and much despised and feared by the Greeks.

APHRODITE
The goddess of love, pleasure, and beauty. She was born in the sea and floated ashore on a large scallop shell. She was beloved by many mortals and gods alike.

HEPHAESTUS
The god of fire, metal-work, stonemasons, and artisans. He made the weapons for the gods on Olympus.

HERMES
The god of travelers, merchants, and thieves. He was also the messenger between gods and men. He was clever and cunning, a poet and orator, and protector of herdsmen and their flocks.

DIONYSUS
The god of wine, feasting, and celebration and patron of the theater. He was the only Olympian born to a mortal mother.

HESTIA
The goddess of the home, family, the hearth, archi-tecture, and the state. She maintained the hearth fire on Mount Olympus, and was known for her kindness.

HADES
The god of the underworld, the dead, and of the riches of the earth—metals and fertile soil. Ancient Greeks feared to speak his name aloud.

The ancient Greeks believed that twelve gods and goddesses ruled the universe—Zeus, the king of the gods, Hera, Poseidon, Demeter, Athena, Artemis, Apollo, Aphrodite, Ares, Hephaestus, Hermes, and either Hestia or Dionysus. Hades, the lord of the underworld, is almost never depicted in the Greek Pantheon because he lived in the underworld and rarely visited Mount Olympus, the tallest mountain in Greece.

With one exception, the Olympians were all related to one another. Zeus, Hera, Poseidon, Demeter, Hades, and Hestia were siblings. Zeus married Hera, and together they were the parents of Ares and Hephaestus. Zeus had many affairs with minor goddesses and mortal women, which resulted in the births of Athena, the twins Artemis and Apollo, Hermes, and Dionysus. Aphrodite is the only Olympian whose parentage was unknown.

AUTHOR'S NOTE

The Greek myths have always attracted me with their power, scope, and imaginativeness, and their possibilities of visual expression. I enjoyed working on an earlier myth, *The Hero and the Minotaur*, the story of young Theseus and the half-man, half-bull minotaur. I was familiar with Jason and the Argonauts from the 1960s film with amazing special effects by Ray Harryhausen. I loved the celebrated stop-motion scene with dueling skeletons and Argonauts, and I was quite disappointed to find out it doesn't exist in the real myth, and I couldn't use it. And I loved the title, *Jason and the Argonauts*!

They were the first superheroes, the first explorers, like ancient astronauts venturing out into the far reaches of their universe, traveling into the unknown. The legends of King Arthur and the Holy Grail, and the saga of the Lord of the Rings would follow this heroic and epic tradition in later Western literature. In these stories heroes are asked to perform a series of seemingly impossible tasks before they can achieve the ultimate reward of the quest.

The myths may seem fictional to us but to the ancient Greeks they were real, and of a religious nature, and needed to reflect what was believed at that time. But as the stories passed down through generations, liberties were taken. In many of the stories there are variations of people's names, dates, locations, and sometimes in the story lines. Even the names and number of Argonauts are contested, as many ancient authors were anxious to include their own ancestors as members of the expedition.

I read every telling of the story I could from contemporary picture books like *D'Aulaires' Book of Greek Myths*, to Hawthorne's *Tanglewood Tales*, and Padraic Colum's *The Golden Fleece and the Heroes Who Lived Before Achilles*. I read Robert Graves's *The Greek Myths*, and his novel, *Hercules, My Shipmate*. The oldest material I used was from Apollonius Rhodius, in his third century B.C. *The Argonautica*. My reference sources for the illustrations were from Internet images and photographs and my personal library and the library from the University of the Arts. My version of the ship the *Argo* was derived from drawings and diagrams of Greek ships of the period, probably around 3,300 years ago.

I have taken what I thought were the most interesting and important episodes from these interpretations, and in the end, I hope I have done them justice and provided a good story and pictures, worthy of those who have told it before I have.

BIBLIOGRAPHY

Colum, Padraic. *The Golden Fleece and the Heroes Who Lived Before Achilles*. New York: Macmillan Publishing Company, 1921.

D'Aulaire, Ingri and Edgar Parin d'Aulaire. *D'Aulaires' Book of Greek Myths*. New York: Bantam Doubleday Dell Publishing Group, Inc., 1962.

Encyclopedia Mythica. "Greek Mythology." Accessed December 3, 2015. http://www.pantheon.org/areas/mythology/europe/greek.

Graves, Robert. *The Greek Myths*, Volume 2. 1955. New York: Penguin Books, 1990.

———. *Hercules, My Shipmate*. New York: American Book-Stratford Press, Inc., 1945.

Hamilton, Edith. *Mythology: Timeless Tales of Gods and Heroes*. Boston: Little, Brown & Company, 1940.

Hawthorne, Nathaniel. *Tanglewood Tales: The Golden Fleece*. New York, Viking Press, 1982.

Morford, Mark, and Robert J. Lenardon. *Classical Mythology*. New York: Longman, Inc., 1971.

Public Broadcasting Service. "Myths: Jason and the Argonauts." Accessed December 3, 2015. http://www.pbs.org/mythsandheroes/myths_four_jason.html.

Smith, Neil. *Myths and Legends: Jason and the Argonauts*. Oxford: Osprey Publishing Ltd., 2013.

IMPORTANT VISUAL SOURCES FOR ILLUSTRATIONS

Maggi, Stefano. *Greece: History and Treasures of an Ancient Civilization*. New York: Sterling Publishing, 2007.

Time-Life Books, *Great Ages of Man*, editor, Bowra, C. M. *Classical Greece*. Time-Life, pub. New York, N.Y. 1965 (important photo and architectural reference)

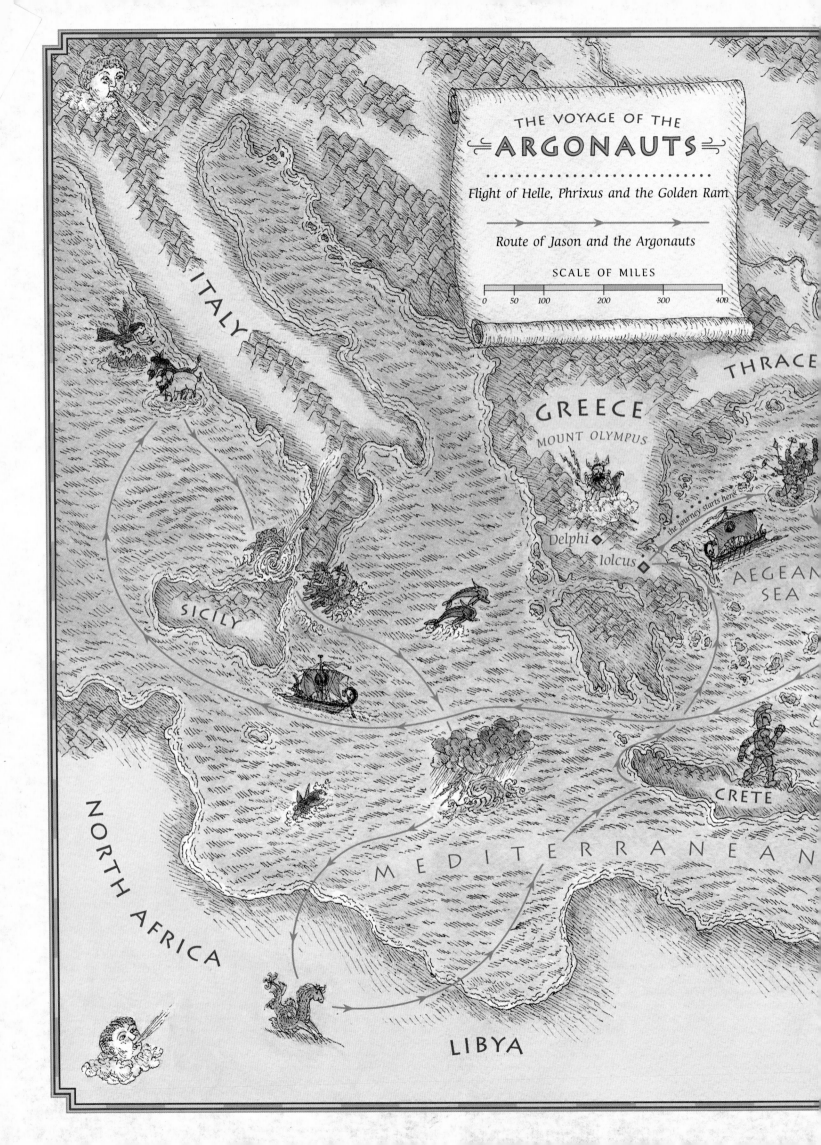

THE VOYAGE OF THE

ARGONAUTS

· ·

Flight of Helle, Phrixus and the Golden Ram

Route of Jason and the Argonauts

SCALE OF MILES

0   50   100   200   300   400

ITALY

THRACE

GREECE

MOUNT OLYMPUS

Delphi

Iolcus

the journey starts here

AEGEAN SEA

SICILY

CRETE

NORTH AFRICA

M E D I T E R R A N E A N

LIBYA